# INCARCERATED

## ACKNOWLEDGMENTS

THE CREATOR OF THE HEAVENS AND EARTH

My Amazing Husband

Our Beautiful Daughters

Our Wonderful Parents

Sol's Write House

# INCARCERATED

This personalized and informative
journal
belongs to:

_____

Welcome to **Love Incarcerated** a personalized and informative journal based on my support group for families, in particular prison wives, fiancéesand girlfriends. This journal will help all womenstepping out on _faith_ to follow their dreams of _hope_ with the _love_ of their life, stayfocused and keep a handle on life. I'm so excited to share this labor of love with my courageous, loving and strong _Q_ueens.

I personally understand that this life can be trying. There are days we feel there's no one to turn to, I wanted to make this journal for you to write out your deepest feelings, enjoy!

INCARCERATED

# Proverbs 31 verses 10 - 31

## Epilogue: The Wife of Noble Character

**10** A wife of noble character who can find? She is worth far more than rubies.

**11** Her husband has full confidence in her and lacks nothing of value.

**12** She brings him goodness, not harm, all the days of her life.

**13** She selects wool and flax and works with eager hands.

**14** She is like the merchant ships, bringing her food from afar.

**15** She gets up while it is still night; she provides food for her family and portions for her female servants.

**16** She considers a field and buys it; out of her earnings she plants a vineyard.

**17** She sets about her work vigorously; her arms are strong for her tasks.

**18** She sees that her trading is profitable, and her lamp does not go out at night.

**19** In her hand she holds the distaff and grasps the spindle with her fingers.

**20** She opens her arms to the poor and extends her hands to the needy.

21 When it snows, she has no fear for her household; for all of them are clothed in scarlet.

22 She makes coverings for her bed; she is clothed in fine linen and purple.

23 Her husband is respected at the city gate, where he takes his seat among the elders of the land.

24 She makes linen garments and sells them, and supplies the merchants with sashes.

25 She is clothed with strength and dignity; she can laugh at the days to come.

26 She speaks with wisdom, and faithful instruction is on her tongue.

27 She watches over the affairs of her household and does not eat the bread of idleness.

28 Her children arise and call her blessed; her husband also, and he praises her:

29 "Many women do noble things, but you surpass them all."

30 Charm is deceptive, and beauty is fleeting; but a woman who fears the LORD is to be praised.

31 Honor her for all that her hands have done, and let her works bring her praise at the city gate.

## The day we first met as recalled by my Husband,

## Shervon "Goldie" Johnson

Love, I know that me being in this place and you in the free world is hard on the both of us. I commend you for being a very strong woman and I love you so much for hanging in there with me.

Love, I remember when I first saw you; I knew I had to have you. It seemed like you were moving in slow motion, your beauty was impeccable, and I knew I had to have you.

Your body and skin tone were perfect, with thighs and legs that would make a grown man beg. Pretty face, pretty smile and some things were just different 'bout you from the rest of the Walter P. females.  You were set apart.

Although, you were the one that got away, in my heart every time I saw you, I knew one day you'd be mine.

I remember the day I first saw you so clearly...you were walking to work the spring of '93.  We already kind of knew each other, so when I caught up with you, you told me you were on your way to work, so I walked with you.  We got to know each other better and I asked you, "Could we chill sometimes"?

You said. "Yes"! I guess shortly after that, maybe a few days or a week, I took you to the movies, it was you and me, my cousin, and his girl, Mandy from Alcoa (R.I.P).

After that we ended up at my granny's house.  It was on a Sunday, with plenty of the family over there. I introduced you to my granny – can't remember all of what was said, but you werewell received. We were both young and you were already in a relationship, but it didn't stop me fromtrying to get with you, but you werelost in the sauce at the time. We still hooked up a couple of times...kissing and hunching, but we never had sex. June 9, 1993, I got locked up for 6 months.  I got outDec. 13, 1993 and didn't see you again until the summer of '94.

You were with someone and I was with someone.  I saw you a few more times but we just stood off and stared at each other. I thought you were so beautiful and sexy with that personality that I always dig. I got into some trouble and went to prison. I thought of you numerous times but each time you were in a relationship. I now look back at every missed opportunity asthe Creator of the heavens and earth perfect timing; I love you, Mrs. Johnson.

Mr. & Mrs. Shervon "Goldie" Johnson
Married:  November 2, 2019
at
Northeast Correctional Complex

INCARCERATED

# What's your version of the day you met your love one?

1. Did someone introduce you?
2. Are you Pen pals, if so what kept you in touch?
3. Did you meet on the internet?
4. Did you already know him (like my relationship)?

**Here's where the pen flows...**

By My *King's* Side

I'm a prison wife. I am not desperate, lonesome, or unattractive. I am strong, educated, independent and beautiful. Let me start by saying that you can love someone in prison, just as you can in the free world. And even more so, yes, he can truly love you. I am my husband's peace and he is mine. I am what take his mind off being in prison. He is what takes my mind off the stresses of the world. At first, I was reluctant, especially with him being in prison for more than 20 plus years. The stories I have heard and having seen women go through being scammed and cheated; I didn't want anything to do with his kind. When I reunited with Goldie, all he asked is that I communicate with him.

After I agreed to let him call me in January 2018, we also began writing each other letters. His letters were full of hopes, dreams, and finding a loyal wife. After several months of writing and talking on the phone, we decided to see each other in person. We agreed that after our first visit, if we weren't feeling anything for each other, we would just keep in touch as friends.

April 22, 2018 was our first visit, and when he walked into the visitation area, I felt a joy come over my body that had my soul whispering to me,

"There he is"! He held me tight and close with his strong arms and I knew we would be more than just friends.

I love Shervon "Goldie" Johnson. We have grown to appreciate one another. He is a true gentleman...my husband is amazing. He brings the best out in me.*Chivalry is NOT dead.* But above all he is compassionate and expresses genuine concern for my wellbeing.

He is respectful, honest and loyal which is a mannerism I forgot men possessed. For me, he is my perfect man. I have learned to love him beyond any worldly pleasures; something that I thought should be a man's priority.

Reunited, falling in love and marrying Goldie while incarcerated has forced us to get to know each other on a level that I have never experienced before. We bothsought to determine if it was the Creator of the heavens and earth will for us to marry. Under the guidance and blessings of our parents and pastor, we concentrated on developing a deep friendship that led us to marriage.

Despite my husband being incarcerated, the barriers of intimacy, family involvement and financial contribution, are maintained by putting the Creator of the heavens and earth first, which provides us a healthy, emotional, intimate relationship but not without frustration.

This life is not for the weak, it requires patience, unconditional love and faith. This journal is a way for you to keep a handle on life while we hold down our incarcerated love ones.

I N C A R C E R A T E D

# Be *joyful*
## in hope
# *patient*
## in affliction
# *faithful*
## in prayer.

Romans 12:12

When seeking justice for your love one, write letters send e-mails and make phone calls. During my husband's incarceration, we learned that U.S. Code 924(c) has been amended and this information is very beneficial to his case. I wrote letters to receive justification to what that meant for his case and found out his received 2 Jail Time Credits which will get him home to me sooner.

ACLU
(American Civil Liberties Union)
125 Broad Street, 18th Floor
New York NY 10004
212-549-2500

BOP
(Federal Bureau of Prisons)
320 First St., NW
Washington, DC 20534
(202) 307-3198

U.S. Department of Justice
950 Pennsylvania of Justice
Washington, DC 20530-0001
Comment Line: 202-353-1555
Main Switchboard: 202-514-2000

**Federal Time Served**: 972-352-4400*(FED's ONLY)* to find how much time your incarcerated love ones have left or how much time they have to do.

Letters to the Department of Justice, including the Attorney General can be sent to this address. The letters will be forwarded to the responsible Dept. of Justice area for appropriate handling.

Also, send your incarcerated love one copies of the letter(s).
This lets your love one know they have your love and support they can count on.

Word of Advice:  Go to your local town councilmen, mayor, senators, congressman, governor, local leaders, and organization that could help. Get as many as possible to write a letter or some formal action on behalf of your request for your love one.  Depending on your area and whose who, a lot of these people can get you the help you need. It helps if...your love one has references, education certificates or anything to make them look good.  Get copies of the things they complete in prison as proof for everyone you talk to.  Also be of good encouragement and work with your love one to set goals for accomplishments.

**Another word of advice**:  Don't waste peoples times or yours by asking people to back you on blind faith alone.  It's good to have something you can show that would get peoples support.
Check out your state for information that would be helpful in supporting your love one.


**TIP:**  If you ever want to check on the well-being of your loveone, call the prison Chaplain.  The Chaplain can do a wellness check and will call you back with an update.

INCARCERATED

## Letters Written To Officals This Year

| To | Date | Response |
|---|---|---|
|  |  |  |
|  |  |  |
|  |  |  |
|  |  |  |
|  |  |  |
|  |  |  |
|  |  |  |
|  |  |  |
|  |  |  |

$$$ Saving Tip:

# H

ere is an affordable way to receive collect calls from your love one.
It's called Google Voice; it allows users to sign up for free and choose
from a list of numbers.  This number is then forwarded to an existing number
(your number) which can be both a landline and a cell phone.

Several people are starting to take advantage of this, so numbers in
select locations may be limited.  You will need to sign up for a number that's local
to the facility, if a number with the area code is not available,
I would wait and check back or you can choose a number close to the facility
surrounding area.  You can find the facilities telephone number
on their website or on the list that I provided.
The first thing you will need to do is sign up for a Google account.
If you have a G-mail account then you already have a Google account
and can just use it to sign up for Google Voice.

## What you need to use Google Voice
- A Google Account
- Computer or mobile phone with internet access (for sign-up)

Sign up for Voice and get your number:**Android device**
Make sure your phone is on and you can get texts. To check, we'll send your
phone a text with a code.

1. On your Android device, download the Google Voice app.
2. Sign into your Google account.
3. After reviewing the Terms of Service and Privacy Policy, tap Continue.
4. Search by city or area code for a number.
5. Next to the number you want, tap Select

Sign up for Voice and get your number:**Computer**

1. On your computer, go to voice.google.com.
2. Sign into your Google Account.
3. After reviewing the Terms of Service and Privacy Policy, tap Continue.
4. Search by city or area code for a number.
5. Next to the number you want, click Select

Sign up for Voice and get your number:  **iPhone & iPad**

Make sure your phone is on and can get texts. To verify, we'll send your phone a text message with a code.

1. On your iPhone or iPad, download the Google Voice app.
2. Sign into your Google Account.
3. After reviewing the Terms of Service and Privacy Policy, tap Accept.
4. Search by city or area code for a number
5. Next to the number you want, tap Select.

## Guidelines to marrying your incarcerated love one

1. The marriage must be approved by the Warden.
2. You and your love one must each submit a letter to the institutional chaplain notifying them of your intent to marry. You, have to mail your letter directly to the chaplain and your love one has a procedure they will follow to get this information to the chaplain.

   a. **Example of Intent to Marry**

   Your Full Name:

   Date of Birth:

   Address:

   I, _____ submit this document as an official request to marry Mr._____ #; D.O.B _____. He is an inmate at _____ (Prison) in _____, (State). This is my sworn statement to confirm that I do not have any legal bindings or restrictions, unresolved marriages, including Common Law, or otherwise that would prohibit marriage to Mr. _____.

   Mr. _____and I have agreed upon an approximate date for our wedding, which is _____.

   We have also agreed to delegate as our ceremony officiate:

   Officiates Name

   Officiates Address:

   Officiates Phone:

   Sincerely,

3. The chaplain completes the Marriage Application, then
4. You will receive instructions from the chaplain to get your paperwork notarized and info about the marriage certificate.
5. Gather names and information of guests, provide this and suggested info to the chaplain no later than 14 days prior to the scheduled wedding. This includes information of outside officiate. The prison chaplain may have a list of officiates for you to use. **Advised everyone of Prison Dress Code.**
6. The letters must be received by the chaplain at least 120 days in advance of the requested wedding date to allow for verification and arrangements. **Granted there are no lockdowns or other incidents.**
7. The chaplain arranges at least four counseling sessions prior to the marriage. The chaplain may conduct the counseling sessions; however, it is permissible for outside ministers/counselors to conduct the sessions upon your love one's request or decision of the chaplain.
8. You must be on your love one's approved visitor list.
9. Prior to the wedding:
    a. The chaplain/counselor will:
        i. Provide your love one's criminal history to you and discuss sentencing and release with both parties
        ii. Review institutional guidelines for the marriage services
        iii. Your love one will prepare and have notarized a statement containing his/her name, age, current address, and the name and address of his/her next of kin or legal guardian. You will need to take this notarized statement to the appropriate court clerk when applying for the marriage license.
10. If the inmate is transferred during the waiting period, the previously approved date of the marriage shall remain in effect.
11. The Warden develops procedures covering marriage ceremonies consistent with the security needs of the institution. At a minimum, these

procedures shall be available to the inmate population and include provisions concerning:

    a.  Permissible locations within the institution for the ceremony

    b.  Application procedures for ceremony

    c.  A brief special visit (1 hour) following the ceremony. The visit will be closely supervised in the same manner as routine visitation.

12. Wedding Ceremony

    a.  The wedding ceremony will consist of your love one and you. The warden may approve four guests from outside of the institution; immediate family only.

    b.  Your love one is required to wear the standard prison issue uniform

13. No items can be brought to the facility for the ceremony, i.e. cake, drinks, non-alcoholic or alcoholic, camera, bouquet, etc. and there will be no reception permitted.

14. It's your responsibility to arrange and pay for all marriage counseling fees, wedding ceremony officiate fees, and licenses. No fees are to be paid to the chaplain and/or institution for services rendered.

15. No free-world money may be brought into the institution during the pre-marital sessions or wedding.

EVERY *love story* IS BEAUTIFUL BUT OURS IS MY FAVORITE

## My Journey to the Prison on my Wedding Day

To be in love with and also marry an inmate, in prison is a task within itself. No one dreams of being with someone behind bars to spend happily ever after with.  My vision certainly wasn't a two hour drive with my brother, my husband's brother, his mother and our pastor at 5:30am on a cold November morning. Nor did it include the presence of Northeast Correctional Complex Saturday morning visitation audience as our witnesses.  But what one usually would not do, you will for love.

Quality time with him was not imagined as time guarded visits sneaking forbidden touches while correctional officers hover around the room.

Personally, before I met my husband, I heard the scandalous stories of women falling in love with an inmate for reasons that they are affectionate and pay attention, attributes of a man that women find hard to resist.  For me, Goldie was familiar and we had history.  But little did I know that when dealing with an inmate, it takes time and money.  I visit with my husband at least 4 times a month.My husband has been incarcerated for 20 plus years and most of those years were NOT with me. The stories that this man has, he could write a book (matter fact, he is). But now he has me, green to the game and I never had been in a situation where I took care of a man, I quickly learned my husband is not just an inmate, he's a survivor.

This life is not for the weak, the smallest misunderstanding goes into an argument and accusations of betrayal. Those days can be draining and questioning but no matter what we went through leading up to that point, visits are a **must**.

Words can never say what I feel, when that man, my husband walks through those visitation doors, its love all over again.

From that moment till they call visiting hours are over, we both know time is of the essence for us to show one another shameless love.

# Visiting with your Love One

*Answers to some questions & other helpful tips*

The first time I went to visit, it was frustrating, confusing and a frightening experience. I wasn't sure of what the process would be like and many questions entered my mind like, what can I wear? What can I bring? Can my daughters come? What ID do I need to present?

## Types of Visitation

1. **Video visitation** can be done from the comfort of your own home. Video visitation works similar to the way you would use Face time or Zoom.

2. **Non-contact or telephone** visitation is when you're separated by glass, but talk on a phone to one another.

3. **Contact visitation** is when you're able to sit at a table. Although contact can occur between you and your love one, you're limited to how much touching can take place.

## Before Your Visit

Make sure that you are on your Love One's visitors list. At some facilities, inmate fills out a list of 10 or so visitors that can visit. Love One's will need to know the visitors full name, address, phone number and sometimes more information. If you think your inmate may not know all this information, you should mail them a letter, or tell them the next time they call. The facility where my husband is requires all prospective visitors to fill out a visitation form that needs to be notarized with a picture.

## The Visitation Form

Visitation forms must be filed out with your name, address, and asks questions such as are you a convicted felon, have you been incarcerated or worked in the department of corrections. Answer the questions truthfully, they use the information to do a background check, and make a decision if you are approved or denied visitation.

Some reasons why your visiting form may be denied are as follows:

- You provided false information

- You are a convicted felon
- You have worked in the department of corrections
- You have outstanding warrants
- You have a protective order out against you or the inmate
- You are deemed a security risk by the facility
- You are on probation, or parole (some exceptions can be made to this)
- You are on another inmate's visitation list at the same institution

Facilities will not inform you of your applications status, they leave it up to your love one to inform you if you were approved or denied or you can call that facility. If you are denied visitation some states let you appeal the decision, however the appeal must be filed within a certain time frame.

## Preparing for Your Visit

Check your love ones' facility schedule for the visitation hours. You can call or check the webpage of the facility to make sure visitationhas not been canceled for any reason, as visiting hours can change or canceled at any time without notice.  A correctional facility may cancel visiting if the facility goes on lockdown, if an inmate has escapes, etc.  Also, if an inmate is in solitary, or 'the hole', their visiting privilege becomes suspended.

Once you know the visiting hours, and have planned which day you will be going, make sure to have proper identification with you.  General a valid state issued photo ID or photo driver's license will do but check the requirements to that facility.

## Visiting with Minors

When visiting with minors or children you'll have to fill out a minor's authorization form attached with a school issued photo ID or birth certificate. Minors are never allowed to go alone to visitation, and must be accompanied by a parent or guardian.

## Dress Code

Staff will reject you from visiting if you violate the dress code, here are the general rules:

- Do not wear clothing that resembles the inmate's clothes, or staff's clothes.  Check with that facility.
- Shirts and shoes are mandatory
- No clothing exposingchest, back, thighs, midsection
- Nothing See through
- No Sleeveless shirts
- No shorts or skirts that are above the knee, no slits above the knee
- No offensive pictures, language on clothing
- No tight clothing, spandex, tank tops, leggings, or tights

**Tip**: *Bring a change of clothing and leave it in your car, this way if you're wearing is a violation of the dress code you can change.*

## Arrival at the Facility and Search

Do not arrive earlier than your facility allows.  Upon arrival to the facility parking lot, your car may be search and everything in it searched by staff, and sometimes canine units (dogs). Once you enter the facility you will be searched again, by pat down and metal detector.  If you refuse to be searched you can be banned from visiting.  In some instances, people are asked to be strip search; a person can refuse, check with the facility and know the consequences and your rights.  Some facilities used ion scanners, that can pick up on small particles of drugs being present but those are not used so much anymore.

## What Items Can You Bring to Visitation?

In general, you can only bring your ID, single car key, eyeglasses (for medical), small bills for the vending machines that are in the visitation room (highly recommend this because you can buy your love one snacks while you visit).  If you have a small child or baby you're allowed to bring a single bottle and diapers. You should never bring medications, cigarettes, or any illegal substances to visitation as this can be cause for a denied visit and possible criminal charges.

What was your 1st prison visit like going to see your love one?

_____

_____

_____

_____

_____

_____

_____

_____

_____

_____

_____

_____

_____

_____

_____

_____

_____

_____

_____

_____

_____

_____

_____

_____

_____

_____

_____

_____

_____

_____

_____

_____

I know...
I know...
the stress and not knowing is a lot to deal with,
but...
be honest with yourself and set boundaries upfront with what you can and cannot
not do.

INCARCERATED

# Month of _____

| Sunday | Monday | Tuesday | Wednesday | Thursday | Friday | Saturday |
|--------|--------|---------|-----------|----------|--------|----------|
|        |        |         |           |          |        |          |
|        |        |         |           |          |        |          |
|        |        |         |           |          |        |          |
|        |        |         |           |          |        |          |
|        |        |         |           |          |        |          |

# Weekly Plan

| | |
|---|---|
| **Sunday** | |
| **Monday** | |
| **Tuesday** | |
| **Wednesday** | |
| **Thursday** | |
| **Friday** | |
| **Saturday** | |

Week of: _____

## Goals

1. _____
2. _____
3. _____
4. _____

## To-Do

○ _____
○ _____
○ _____
○ _____
○ _____
○ _____
○ _____
○ _____

## Notes

_____
_____
_____
_____

# Weekly Plan

| | |
|---|---|
| **Sunday** | |
| **Monday** | |
| **Tuesday** | |
| **Wednesday** | |
| **Thursday** | |
| **Friday** | |
| **Saturday** | |

Week of: _____

## Goals

1. _____
2. _____
3. _____
4. _____

## To-Do

○ _____
○ _____
○ _____
○ _____
○ _____
○ _____
○ _____
○ _____

## Notes

_____
_____
_____
_____

# Weekly Plan

| | |
|---|---|
| Sunday | |
| Monday | |
| Tuesday | |
| Wednesday | |
| Thursday | |
| Friday | |
| Saturday | |

Week of: _____

## Goals

1. _____
2. _____
3. _____
4. _____

## To-Do

- ○ _____
- ○ _____
- ○ _____
- ○ _____
- ○ _____
- ○ _____
- ○ _____
- ○ _____

## Notes

_____
_____
_____
_____

# Weekly Plan

| | |
|---|---|
| Sunday | |
| Monday | |
| Tuesday | |
| Wednesday | |
| Thursday | |
| Friday | |
| Saturday | |

Week of: _____

## Goals

1. _____
2. _____
3. _____
4. _____

## To-Do

○ _____
○ _____
○ _____
○ _____
○ _____
○ _____
○ _____
○ _____

## Notes

_____
_____
_____
_____

Date:

How was visit with your love one?

_____

_____

_____

_____

_____

_____

_____

_____

_____

_____

_____

_____

_____

_____

_____

_____

Date:

How was visit with your love one?

_____

_____

_____

_____

_____

_____

_____

_____

_____

_____

_____

_____

_____

_____

_____

_____

_____

# my prayer
### LIST

*family*
_____
_____
_____
_____

*friends*
_____
_____
_____
_____

*neighbors*
_____
_____
_____
_____

*self*
_____
_____
_____
_____

# Relationship Building
## Shared Qualities

### We would like to visit:

1 _____

2 _____

3 _____

### Movies, books, or music we like:

1 _____

2 _____

3 _____

### We have fun when we:

1 _____

2 _____

3 _____

### As a couple, we're good at:

1 _____

2 _____

3 _____

### As a couple, our weaknesses are:

1 _____

2 _____

3 _____

### Unique things we have in common:

1 _____

2 _____

3 _____

### Qualities we value in a person:

1 _____

2 _____

3 _____

### Three goals for our future:

1 _____

2 _____

3 _____

# Month of _____

| Sunday | Monday | Tuesday | Wednesday | Thursday | Friday | Saturday |
|--------|--------|---------|-----------|----------|--------|----------|
|        |        |         |           |          |        |          |
|        |        |         |           |          |        |          |
|        |        |         |           |          |        |          |
|        |        |         |           |          |        |          |
|        |        |         |           |          |        |          |

# Weekly Plan

| | |
|---|---|
| **Sunday** | |
| **Monday** | |
| **Tuesday** | |
| **Wednesday** | |
| **Thursday** | |
| **Friday** | |
| **Saturday** | |

Week of: _____

## Goals

1. _____
2. _____
3. _____
4. _____

## To-Do

○ _____
○ _____
○ _____
○ _____
○ _____
○ _____
○ _____
○ _____

## Notes

_____
_____
_____
_____

# Weekly Plan

| | |
|---|---|
| **Sunday** | |
| **Monday** | |
| **Tuesday** | |
| **Wednesday** | |
| **Thursday** | |
| **Friday** | |
| **Saturday** | |

Week of: _____

## Goals

1. _____
2. _____
3. _____
4. _____

## To-Do

○ _____
○ _____
○ _____
○ _____
○ _____
○ _____
○ _____
○ _____

## Notes

_____
_____
_____
_____

# Weekly Plan

| | |
|---|---|
| **Sunday** | |
| **Monday** | |
| **Tuesday** | |
| **Wednesday** | |
| **Thursday** | |
| **Friday** | |
| **Saturday** | |

Week of: _____

## Goals

1. _____
2. _____
3. _____
4. _____

## To-Do

○ _____
○ _____
○ _____
○ _____
○ _____
○ _____
○ _____
○ _____

## Notes

_____
_____
_____
_____

# Weekly Plan

| | |
|---|---|
| Sunday | |
| Monday | |
| Tuesday | |
| Wednesday | |
| Thursday | |
| Friday | |
| Saturday | |

Week of: _____

## Goals

1. _____
2. _____
3. _____
4. _____

## To-Do

○ _____
○ _____
○ _____
○ _____
○ _____
○ _____
○ _____
○ _____

## Notes

_____
_____
_____
_____

Date:

How was visit with your love one?

_____

_____

_____

_____

_____

_____

_____

_____

_____

_____

_____

_____

_____

_____

_____

_____

_____

_____

Date:

How was visit with your love one?

_____

_____

_____

_____

_____

_____

_____

_____

_____

_____

_____

_____

_____

_____

_____

# my prayer LIST

family

_____
_____
_____
_____

friends

_____
_____
_____
_____

neighbors

_____
_____
_____
_____

self

_____
_____
_____
_____

# 5 Spoken Acts of Love

## 1. Words of affirmation
- ♥ I love how...
- ♥ You look...
- ♥ I really like how you...
- ♥ Thank you for...

## 2. Quality Time
Giving your love undivided attention:
- ♥ No TV& No Phone
- ♥ Talking and listening
- ♥ Taking a walk together while holding hands

## 3. Celebrate one another with thoughtful gifts
- ♥ Gifts are a kind gesture of appreciation
- ♥ Be creative and have fun

## 4. Acts of Kindness
- ♥ Preparing breakfast, lunch or dinner for one another
- ♥ Picking up some of your partners responsibilities
- ♥ to lessen the stress(when the time comes)

## 5. Physical Touch
- ♥ Holding hands
- ♥ Simple hug (especially the ones from behind)

It is said that the physical act of a kind and warm touch lowers the blood pressure and releases the "love hormone", oxytocin.

# Month of _____

| Sunday | Monday | Tuesday | Wednesday | Thursday | Friday | Saturday |
|--------|--------|---------|-----------|----------|--------|----------|
|        |        |         |           |          |        |          |
|        |        |         |           |          |        |          |
|        |        |         |           |          |        |          |
|        |        |         |           |          |        |          |
|        |        |         |           |          |        |          |

# Weekly Plan

| | |
|---|---|
| **Sunday** | |
| **Monday** | |
| **Tuesday** | |
| **Wednesday** | |
| **Thursday** | |
| **Friday** | |
| **Saturday** | |

Week of: _____

## Goals

1. _____
2. _____
3. _____
4. _____

## To-Do

○ _____
○ _____
○ _____
○ _____
○ _____
○ _____
○ _____
○ _____

## Notes

_____
_____
_____
_____

# Weekly Plan

| | |
|---|---|
| **Sunday** | |
| **Monday** | |
| **Tuesday** | |
| **Wednesday** | |
| **Thursday** | |
| **Friday** | |
| **Saturday** | |

Week of: _____

## Goals

1. _____
2. _____
3. _____
4. _____

## To-Do

○ _____
○ _____
○ _____
○ _____
○ _____
○ _____
○ _____
○ _____

## Notes

_____
_____
_____
_____

# Weekly Plan

| | |
|---|---|
| **Sunday** | |
| **Monday** | |
| **Tuesday** | |
| **Wednesday** | |
| **Thursday** | |
| **Friday** | |
| **Saturday** | |

Week of: _____

## Goals

1. _____
2. _____
3. _____
4. _____

## To-Do

○ _____
○ _____
○ _____
○ _____
○ _____
○ _____
○ _____
○ _____

## Notes

_____
_____
_____
_____

# Weekly Plan

| | |
|---|---|
| Sunday | |
| Monday | |
| Tuesday | |
| Wednesday | |
| Thursday | |
| Friday | |
| Saturday | |

Week of: _____

## Goals

1. _____
2. _____
3. _____
4. _____

## To-Do

○ _____
○ _____
○ _____
○ _____
○ _____
○ _____
○ _____
○ _____

## Notes

_____
_____
_____
_____

Date:

How was visit with your love one?

_____

_____

_____

_____

_____

_____

_____

_____

_____

_____

_____

_____

_____

_____

_____

_____

Date:

How was visit with your love one?

_____

_____

_____

_____

_____

_____

_____

_____

_____

_____

_____

_____

_____

_____

_____

_____

# my prayer
## LIST

family

_____
_____
_____
_____

friends

_____
_____
_____
_____

neighbors

_____
_____
_____
_____

self

_____
_____
_____
_____

## Tips for prison wives, fiancées& girlfriends

♥ Write some letters, while listening to your favorite love songs.
*Get you some colored paper, pens and pencils tell him how it's you and him against the world, blow his mind, get in your feelings, make him feel how much you love and miss them.*
*(Writing can be very therapeutic).*

♥ Don't stress out if they don't call for a day or two.
*You can call the Chaplain; every prison has one and they can check on your love one and get back to you.*
*(Trust and believe if they could, they would, and they will)*

♥ Get to know other families that you see at visit.
*Not saying that you have to be buddy-buddy, but they can be a valuable source of information.*

Most importantly, take care of yourself! Keep in contact with friends, write in your Love Incarcerated Journal, listen to your favorite upbeat music, get out and be sociable, start your own journal. You can learn to start and write your very own journal through Sols Write House, located at 4101 Holston Dr, Knoxville, TN 37914 or call Sherri Williams, Mobile # 865-444-9063, Office # 865-249-8108.
Tell her Mrs. Goldie sent you.

# Month of _____

| Sunday | Monday | Tuesday | Wednesday | Thursday | Friday | Saturday |
|--------|--------|---------|-----------|----------|--------|----------|
|        |        |         |           |          |        |          |
|        |        |         |           |          |        |          |
|        |        |         |           |          |        |          |
|        |        |         |           |          |        |          |
|        |        |         |           |          |        |          |

# Weekly Plan

| |
|---|
| Sunday |
| Monday |
| Tuesday |
| Wednesday |
| Thursday |
| Friday |
| Saturday |

Week of: _____

## Goals

1. _____
2. _____
3. _____
4. _____

## To-Do

○ _____
○ _____
○ _____
○ _____
○ _____
○ _____
○ _____
○ _____

## Notes

_____
_____
_____
_____

# Weekly Plan

| | |
|---|---|
| Sunday | |
| Monday | |
| Tuesday | |
| Wednesday | |
| Thursday | |
| Friday | |
| Saturday | |

Week of: _____

## Goals

1. _____
2. _____
3. _____
4. _____

## To-Do

○ _____
○ _____
○ _____
○ _____
○ _____
○ _____
○ _____
○ _____

## Notes

_____
_____
_____
_____

# Weekly Plan

| Sunday |
|---|
|  |

| Monday |
|---|
|  |

| Tuesday |
|---|
|  |

| Wednesday |
|---|
|  |

| Thursday |
|---|
|  |

| Friday |
|---|
|  |

| Saturday |
|---|
|  |

Week of: _____

## Goals

1. _____
2. _____
3. _____
4. _____

## To-Do

○ _____
○ _____
○ _____
○ _____
○ _____
○ _____
○ _____
○ _____

## Notes

_____
_____
_____
_____

# Weekly Plan

| | |
|---|---|
| **Sunday** | |
| **Monday** | |
| **Tuesday** | |
| **Wednesday** | |
| **Thursday** | |
| **Friday** | |
| **Saturday** | |

Week of: _____

## Goals

1. _____
2. _____
3. _____
4. _____

## To-Do

○ _____
○ _____
○ _____
○ _____
○ _____
○ _____
○ _____
○ _____

## Notes

_____
_____
_____
_____

How was visit with your love one?

_____

_____

_____

_____

_____

_____

_____

_____

_____

_____

_____

_____

_____

_____

_____

_____

Date:

How was visit with your love one?

_____

_____

_____

_____

_____

_____

_____

_____

_____

_____

_____

_____

_____

_____

_____

_____

# my prayer
## LIST

*family*

_____

_____

_____

_____

*friends*

_____

_____

_____

_____

*neighbors*

_____

_____

_____

_____

*self*

_____

_____

_____

_____

# PRAY MORE
*worry less*

# Month of _____

| Sunday | Monday | Tuesday | Wednesday | Thursday | Friday | Saturday |
|--------|--------|---------|-----------|----------|--------|----------|
|        |        |         |           |          |        |          |
|        |        |         |           |          |        |          |
|        |        |         |           |          |        |          |
|        |        |         |           |          |        |          |
|        |        |         |           |          |        |          |

# Weekly Plan

| | |
|---|---|
| **Sunday** | |
| **Monday** | |
| **Tuesday** | |
| **Wednesday** | |
| **Thursday** | |
| **Friday** | |
| **Saturday** | |

Week of: _____

## Goals

1. _____
2. _____
3. _____
4. _____

## To-Do

○ _____
○ _____
○ _____
○ _____
○ _____
○ _____
○ _____
○ _____

## Notes

_____
_____
_____
_____

# Weekly Plan

| | |
|---|---|
| **Sunday** | |
| **Monday** | |
| **Tuesday** | |
| **Wednesday** | |
| **Thursday** | |
| **Friday** | |
| **Saturday** | |

Week of: _____

## Goals

1. _____
2. _____
3. _____
4. _____

## To-Do

○ _____
○ _____
○ _____
○ _____
○ _____
○ _____
○ _____
○ _____

## Notes

_____
_____
_____
_____

# Weekly Plan

| | |
|---|---|
| Sunday | |
| Monday | |
| Tuesday | |
| Wednesday | |
| Thursday | |
| Friday | |
| Saturday | |

Week of: _____

## Goals

1. _____
2. _____
3. _____
4. _____

## To-Do

○ _____
○ _____
○ _____
○ _____
○ _____
○ _____
○ _____
○ _____

## Notes

_____
_____
_____
_____

# Weekly Plan

| | |
|---|---|
| **Sunday** | |
| **Monday** | |
| **Tuesday** | |
| **Wednesday** | |
| **Thursday** | |
| **Friday** | |
| **Saturday** | |

Week of: _____

## Goals

1. _____
2. _____
3. _____
4. _____

## To-Do

- ○ _____
- ○ _____
- ○ _____
- ○ _____
- ○ _____
- ○ _____
- ○ _____
- ○ _____

## Notes

_____
_____
_____
_____

Date:

How was visit with your love one?

_____

_____

_____

_____

_____

_____

_____

_____

_____

_____

_____

_____

_____

_____

_____

Date:

How was visit with your love one?

_____

_____

_____

_____

_____

_____

_____

_____

_____

_____

_____

_____

_____

_____

_____

_____

# my prayer
## LIST

*family*

_____
_____
_____
_____

*friends*

_____
_____
_____
_____

*neighbors*

_____
_____
_____
_____

*self*

_____
_____
_____
_____

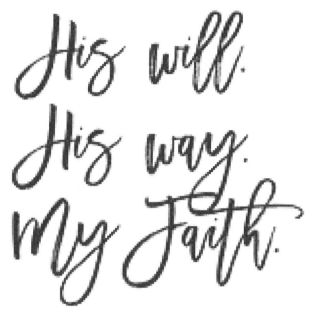

His will.
His way.
My Faith.

JEREMIAH 29:11

# Month of _____

| Sunday | Monday | Tuesday | Wednesday | Thursday | Friday | Saturday |
|--------|--------|---------|-----------|----------|--------|----------|
|        |        |         |           |          |        |          |
|        |        |         |           |          |        |          |
|        |        |         |           |          |        |          |
|        |        |         |           |          |        |          |
|        |        |         |           |          |        |          |

# Weekly Plan

| | |
|---|---|
| Sunday | |
| Monday | |
| Tuesday | |
| Wednesday | |
| Thursday | |
| Friday | |
| Saturday | |

Week of: _____

## Goals

1. _____
2. _____
3. _____
4. _____

## To-Do

○ _____
○ _____
○ _____
○ _____
○ _____
○ _____
○ _____
○ _____

## Notes

_____
_____
_____
_____

# Weekly Plan

| Sunday |
| --- |
| |

| Monday |
| --- |
| |

| Tuesday |
| --- |
| |

| Wednesday |
| --- |
| |

| Thursday |
| --- |
| |

| Friday |
| --- |
| |

| Saturday |
| --- |
| |

Week of: _____

## Goals

1. _____
2. _____
3. _____
4. _____

## To-Do

○ _____
○ _____
○ _____
○ _____
○ _____
○ _____
○ _____
○ _____

## Notes

_____
_____
_____
_____

# Weekly Plan

| | |
|---|---|
| **Sunday** | |
| **Monday** | |
| **Tuesday** | |
| **Wednesday** | |
| **Thursday** | |
| **Friday** | |
| **Saturday** | |

Week of: _____

## Goals

1. _____
2. _____
3. _____
4. _____

## To-Do

○ _____
○ _____
○ _____
○ _____
○ _____
○ _____
○ _____
○ _____

## Notes

_____
_____
_____
_____

# Weekly Plan

| | |
|---|---|
| **Sunday** | |
| **Monday** | |
| **Tuesday** | |
| **Wednesday** | |
| **Thursday** | |
| **Friday** | |
| **Saturday** | |

Week of: _____

## Goals

1. _____
2. _____
3. _____
4. _____

## To-Do

○ _____
○ _____
○ _____
○ _____
○ _____
○ _____
○ _____
○ _____

## Notes

_____
_____
_____
_____

Date:

How was visit with your love one?

_____

_____

_____

_____

_____

_____

_____

_____

_____

_____

_____

_____

_____

_____

_____

_____

Date:

How was visit with your love one?

_____

_____

_____

_____

_____

_____

_____

_____

_____

_____

_____

_____

_____

_____

_____

_____

_____

# my prayer
## LIST

*family*

_____
_____
_____
_____

*friends*

_____
_____
_____
_____

*neighbors*

_____
_____
_____
_____

*self*

_____
_____
_____
_____

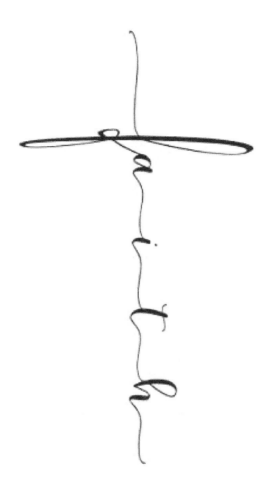

# Month of _____

| Sunday | Monday | Tuesday | Wednesday | Thursday | Friday | Saturday |
|--------|--------|---------|-----------|----------|--------|----------|
|        |        |         |           |          |        |          |
|        |        |         |           |          |        |          |
|        |        |         |           |          |        |          |
|        |        |         |           |          |        |          |
|        |        |         |           |          |        |          |

# Weekly Plan

| | |
|---|---|
| **Sunday** | |
| **Monday** | |
| **Tuesday** | |
| **Wednesday** | |
| **Thursday** | |
| **Friday** | |
| **Saturday** | |

Week of: _____

## Goals

1. _____
2. _____
3. _____
4. _____

## To-Do

○ _____
○ _____
○ _____
○ _____
○ _____
○ _____
○ _____
○ _____

## Notes

_____
_____
_____
_____

# Weekly Plan

| | |
|---|---|
| **Sunday** | |
| **Monday** | |
| **Tuesday** | |
| **Wednesday** | |
| **Thursday** | |
| **Friday** | |
| **Saturday** | |

Week of: _____

## Goals

1. _____
2. _____
3. _____
4. _____

## To-Do

○ _____
○ _____
○ _____
○ _____
○ _____
○ _____
○ _____
○ _____

## Notes

_____
_____
_____
_____

# Weekly Plan

| Sunday | |
|---|---|
| **Monday** | |
| **Tuesday** | |
| **Wednesday** | |
| **Thursday** | |
| **Friday** | |
| **Saturday** | |

Week of: _____

## Goals

1. _____
2. _____
3. _____
4. _____

## To-Do

○ _____
○ _____
○ _____
○ _____
○ _____
○ _____
○ _____
○ _____

## Notes

_____
_____
_____
_____

# Weekly Plan

| | |
|---|---|
| Sunday | |
| Monday | |
| Tuesday | |
| Wednesday | |
| Thursday | |
| Friday | |
| Saturday | |

Week of: _____

## Goals

1. _____
2. _____
3. _____
4. _____

## To-Do

○ _____
○ _____
○ _____
○ _____
○ _____
○ _____
○ _____
○ _____

## Notes

_____
_____
_____
_____

Date:

How was visit with your love one?

_____

_____

_____

_____

_____

_____

_____

_____

_____

_____

_____

_____

_____

_____

_____

_____

Date:

How was visit with your love one?

_____

_____

_____

_____

_____

_____

_____

_____

_____

_____

_____

_____

_____

_____

_____

_____

# my prayer LIST

family

friends

neighbors

self

You put your
Arms around
Me and I'm
Home

# Month of _____

| Sunday | Monday | Tuesday | Wednesday | Thursday | Friday | Saturday |
|--------|--------|---------|-----------|----------|--------|----------|
|        |        |         |           |          |        |          |
|        |        |         |           |          |        |          |
|        |        |         |           |          |        |          |
|        |        |         |           |          |        |          |
|        |        |         |           |          |        |          |

# Weekly Plan

| | |
|---|---|
| **Sunday** | |
| **Monday** | |
| **Tuesday** | |
| **Wednesday** | |
| **Thursday** | |
| **Friday** | |
| **Saturday** | |

Week of: _____

## Goals

1. _____
2. _____
3. _____
4. _____

## To-Do

○ _____
○ _____
○ _____
○ _____
○ _____
○ _____
○ _____
○ _____

## Notes

_____
_____
_____
_____

# Weekly Plan

| | |
|---|---|
| **Sunday** | |
| **Monday** | |
| **Tuesday** | |
| **Wednesday** | |
| **Thursday** | |
| **Friday** | |
| **Saturday** | |

Week of: _____

## Goals

1. _____
2. _____
3. _____
4. _____

## To-Do

○ _____
○ _____
○ _____
○ _____
○ _____
○ _____
○ _____
○ _____

## Notes

_____
_____
_____
_____

# Weekly Plan

Sunday

Monday

Tuesday

Wednesday

Thursday

Friday

Saturday

Week of: _____

## Goals

1. _____
2. _____
3. _____
4. _____

## To-Do

○ _____
○ _____
○ _____
○ _____
○ _____
○ _____
○ _____
○ _____

## Notes

_____
_____
_____
_____

# Weekly Plan

| | |
|---|---|
| Sunday | |
| Monday | |
| Tuesday | |
| Wednesday | |
| Thursday | |
| Friday | |
| Saturday | |

Week of: _____

## Goals

1. _____
2. _____
3. _____
4. _____

## To-Do

○ _____
○ _____
○ _____
○ _____
○ _____
○ _____
○ _____
○ _____

## Notes

_____
_____
_____
_____

Date:

How was visit with your love one?

_____

_____

_____

_____

_____

_____

_____

_____

_____

_____

_____

_____

_____

_____

_____

_____

Date:

How was visit with your love one?

_____

_____

_____

_____

_____

_____

_____

_____

_____

_____

_____

_____

_____

_____

_____

# my prayer
## LIST

*family*

_____
_____
_____
_____

*friends*

_____
_____
_____
_____

*neighbors*

_____
_____
_____
_____

*self*

_____
_____
_____

For *Beautiful Eyes*
look for the good in others, for
*Beautiful Lips*
speak only words of kindness, and
*For Poise*
walk in the knowledge that you are
*Never Alone.*

-Audrey Hepburn

# Month of _____

| Sunday | Monday | Tuesday | Wednesday | Thursday | Friday | Saturday |
|--------|--------|---------|-----------|----------|--------|----------|
|        |        |         |           |          |        |          |
|        |        |         |           |          |        |          |
|        |        |         |           |          |        |          |
|        |        |         |           |          |        |          |
|        |        |         |           |          |        |          |

# Weekly Plan

| | |
|---|---|
| Sunday | |
| Monday | |
| Tuesday | |
| Wednesday | |
| Thursday | |
| Friday | |
| Saturday | |

Week of: _____

## Goals

1. _____
2. _____
3. _____
4. _____

## To-Do

○ _____
○ _____
○ _____
○ _____
○ _____
○ _____
○ _____
○ _____

## Notes

_____
_____
_____
_____

# Weekly Plan

Sunday

Monday

Tuesday

Wednesday

Thursday

Friday

Saturday

Week of: _____

## Goals

1. _____
2. _____
3. _____
4. _____

## To-Do

- ○ _____
- ○ _____
- ○ _____
- ○ _____
- ○ _____
- ○ _____
- ○ _____
- ○ _____

## Notes

_____
_____
_____
_____

# Weekly Plan

| Sunday |
| Monday |
| Tuesday |
| Wednesday |
| Thursday |
| Friday |
| Saturday |

Week of: _____

## Goals

1. _____
2. _____
3. _____
4. _____

## To-Do

○ _____
○ _____
○ _____
○ _____
○ _____
○ _____
○ _____
○ _____

## Notes

_____
_____
_____
_____

# Weekly Plan

| | |
|---|---|
| Sunday | |
| Monday | |
| Tuesday | |
| Wednesday | |
| Thursday | |
| Friday | |
| Saturday | |

Week of: _____

## Goals

1. _____
2. _____
3. _____
4. _____

## To-Do

○ _____
○ _____
○ _____
○ _____
○ _____
○ _____
○ _____
○ _____

## Notes

_____
_____
_____
_____

Date:

How was visit with your love one?

_____

_____

_____

_____

_____

_____

_____

_____

_____

_____

_____

_____

_____

_____

_____

_____

_____

Date:

How was visit with your love one?

_____

_____

_____

_____

_____

_____

_____

_____

_____

_____

_____

_____

_____

_____

_____

_____

# my prayer
## LIST

family

_____

_____

_____

_____

friends

_____

_____

_____

_____

neighbors

_____

_____

_____

_____

self

_____

_____

_____

_____

# Month of _____

| Sunday | Monday | Tuesday | Wednesday | Thursday | Friday | Saturday |
|--------|--------|---------|-----------|----------|--------|----------|
|        |        |         |           |          |        |          |
|        |        |         |           |          |        |          |
|        |        |         |           |          |        |          |
|        |        |         |           |          |        |          |
|        |        |         |           |          |        |          |

# Weekly Plan

| | |
|---|---|
| Sunday | |
| Monday | |
| Tuesday | |
| Wednesday | |
| Thursday | |
| Friday | |
| Saturday | |

Week of: _____

## Goals

1. _____
2. _____
3. _____
4. _____

## To-Do

○ _____
○ _____
○ _____
○ _____
○ _____
○ _____
○ _____
○ _____

## Notes

_____
_____
_____
_____

# Weekly Plan

| Sunday |
|---|
|  |

| Monday |
|---|
|  |

| Tuesday |
|---|
|  |

| Wednesday |
|---|
|  |

| Thursday |
|---|
|  |

| Friday |
|---|
|  |

| Saturday |
|---|
|  |

Week of: _____

## Goals

1. _____
2. _____
3. _____
4. _____

## To-Do

○ _____
○ _____
○ _____
○ _____
○ _____
○ _____
○ _____
○ _____

## Notes

_____
_____
_____
_____

# Weekly Plan

| | |
|---|---|
| **Sunday** | |
| **Monday** | |
| **Tuesday** | |
| **Wednesday** | |
| **Thursday** | |
| **Friday** | |
| **Saturday** | |

Week of: _____

## Goals

1. _____
2. _____
3. _____
4. _____

## To-Do

○ _____
○ _____
○ _____
○ _____
○ _____
○ _____
○ _____
○ _____

## Notes

_____
_____
_____
_____

# Weekly Plan

| | |
|---|---|
| **Sunday** | |
| **Monday** | |
| **Tuesday** | |
| **Wednesday** | |
| **Thursday** | |
| **Friday** | |
| **Saturday** | |

Week of: _____

## Goals

1. _____
2. _____
3. _____
4. _____

## To-Do

○ _____
○ _____
○ _____
○ _____
○ _____
○ _____
○ _____
○ _____

## Notes

_____
_____
_____
_____

Date:

How was visit with your love one?

_____

_____

_____

_____

_____

_____

_____

_____

_____

_____

_____

_____

_____

_____

_____

_____

_____

Date:

How was visit with your love one?

_____

_____

_____

_____

_____

_____

_____

_____

_____

_____

_____

_____

_____

_____

_____

_____

# my prayer
## LIST

family

_____
_____
_____
_____

friends

_____
_____
_____
_____

neighbors

_____
_____
_____
_____

self

_____
_____
_____
_____

**Eros** - a love felt particularly within the body

(Sensual or romantic love)

1. **Philia** - a love of the soul

(Brotherly love)

2. **Agape**- a parental, mature, sacrificial kind of love

(The Creator of the heavens and earth's love for us)

3. **Storge** -This is the love of community and family.

Regardless, the love it's a love that's looked forward to.

Visits are so important to inmates, having contact with a family member or friend provides mental and emotional support for their well-being.

# Month of _____

| Sunday | Monday | Tuesday | Wednesday | Thursday | Friday | Saturday |
|--------|--------|---------|-----------|----------|--------|----------|
|        |        |         |           |          |        |          |
|        |        |         |           |          |        |          |
|        |        |         |           |          |        |          |
|        |        |         |           |          |        |          |
|        |        |         |           |          |        |          |

# Weekly Plan

| | |
|---|---|
| **Sunday** | |
| **Monday** | |
| **Tuesday** | |
| **Wednesday** | |
| **Thursday** | |
| **Friday** | |
| **Saturday** | |

Week of: _____

## Goals

1. _____
2. _____
3. _____
4. _____

## To-Do

- ○ _____
- ○ _____
- ○ _____
- ○ _____
- ○ _____
- ○ _____
- ○ _____
- ○ _____

## Notes

_____
_____
_____
_____

# Weekly Plan

| Sunday |
|---|
|  |

| Monday |
|---|
|  |

| Tuesday |
|---|
|  |

| Wednesday |
|---|
|  |

| Thursday |
|---|
|  |

| Friday |
|---|
|  |

| Saturday |
|---|
|  |

Week of: _____

## Goals

1. _____
2. _____
3. _____
4. _____

## To-Do

○ _____
○ _____
○ _____
○ _____
○ _____
○ _____
○ _____
○ _____

## Notes

_____
_____
_____
_____

# Weekly Plan

| | |
|---|---|
| **Sunday** | |
| **Monday** | |
| **Tuesday** | |
| **Wednesday** | |
| **Thursday** | |
| **Friday** | |
| **Saturday** | |

Week of: _____

## Goals

1. _____
2. _____
3. _____
4. _____

## To-Do

○ _____
○ _____
○ _____
○ _____
○ _____
○ _____
○ _____
○ _____

## Notes

_____
_____
_____
_____

# Weekly Plan

| | |
|---|---|
| **Sunday** | |
| **Monday** | |
| **Tuesday** | |
| **Wednesday** | |
| **Thursday** | |
| **Friday** | |
| **Saturday** | |

Week of: _____

## Goals

1. _____
2. _____
3. _____
4. _____

## To-Do

○ _____
○ _____
○ _____
○ _____
○ _____
○ _____
○ _____
○ _____

## Notes

_____
_____
_____
_____

Date:

How was visit with your love one?

_____

_____

_____

_____

_____

_____

_____

_____

_____

_____

_____

_____

_____

_____

_____

_____

Date:

How was visit with your love one?

_____

_____

_____

_____

_____

_____

_____

_____

_____

_____

_____

_____

_____

_____

_____

_____

# my prayer
## LIST

family
_____
_____
_____
_____

friends
_____
_____
_____
_____

neighbors
_____
_____
_____
_____

self
_____
_____
_____
_____

# ONE DAY

*Someone will walk
into your life and
make you see why
it never worked out
with anyone else*

# Month of _____

| Sunday | Monday | Tuesday | Wednesday | Thursday | Friday | Saturday |
|--------|--------|---------|-----------|----------|--------|----------|
|        |        |         |           |          |        |          |
|        |        |         |           |          |        |          |
|        |        |         |           |          |        |          |
|        |        |         |           |          |        |          |
|        |        |         |           |          |        |          |

# Weekly Plan

| Sunday | |
|---|---|
| **Monday** | |
| **Tuesday** | |
| **Wednesday** | |
| **Thursday** | |
| **Friday** | |
| **Saturday** | |

Week of: _____

## Goals

1. _____
2. _____
3. _____
4. _____

## To-Do

○ _____
○ _____
○ _____
○ _____
○ _____
○ _____
○ _____
○ _____

## Notes

_____
_____
_____
_____

# Weekly Plan

| | |
|---|---|
| Sunday | |
| Monday | |
| Tuesday | |
| Wednesday | |
| Thursday | |
| Friday | |
| Saturday | |

Week of: _____

## Goals

1. _____
2. _____
3. _____
4. _____

## To-Do

- ○ _____
- ○ _____
- ○ _____
- ○ _____
- ○ _____
- ○ _____
- ○ _____
- ○ _____

## Notes

_____
_____
_____
_____

# Weekly Plan

| | |
|---|---|
| **Sunday** | |
| **Monday** | |
| **Tuesday** | |
| **Wednesday** | |
| **Thursday** | |
| **Friday** | |
| **Saturday** | |

Week of: _____

## Goals

1. _____
2. _____
3. _____
4. _____

## To-Do

○ _____
○ _____
○ _____
○ _____
○ _____
○ _____
○ _____
○ _____

## Notes

_____
_____
_____
_____

# Weekly Plan

| | |
|---|---|
| Sunday | |
| Monday | |
| Tuesday | |
| Wednesday | |
| Thursday | |
| Friday | |
| Saturday | |

Week of: _____

## Goals

1. _____
2. _____
3. _____
4. _____

## To-Do

○ _____
○ _____
○ _____
○ _____
○ _____
○ _____
○ _____
○ _____

## Notes

_____
_____
_____
_____

Date:

How was visit with your love one?

_____

_____

_____

_____

_____

_____

_____

_____

_____

_____

_____

_____

_____

_____

_____

_____

Date:

How was visit with your love one?

_____

_____

_____

_____

_____

_____

_____

_____

_____

_____

_____

_____

_____

_____

_____

_____

# my prayer
## LIST

family

_____
_____
_____
_____

friends

_____
_____
_____
_____

neighbors

_____
_____
_____
_____

self

_____
_____
_____
_____

# Month of _____

| Sunday | Monday | Tuesday | Wednesday | Thursday | Friday | Saturday |
| --- | --- | --- | --- | --- | --- | --- |
|  |  |  |  |  |  |  |
|  |  |  |  |  |  |  |
|  |  |  |  |  |  |  |
|  |  |  |  |  |  |  |
|  |  |  |  |  |  |  |

# Weekly Plan

| | |
|---|---|
| **Sunday** | |
| **Monday** | |
| **Tuesday** | |
| **Wednesday** | |
| **Thursday** | |
| **Friday** | |
| **Saturday** | |

Week of: _____

## Goals

1. _____
2. _____
3. _____
4. _____

## To-Do

○ _____
○ _____
○ _____
○ _____
○ _____
○ _____
○ _____
○ _____

## Notes

_____
_____
_____
_____

# Weekly Plan

| Sunday |
|---|
|  |

| Monday |
|---|
|  |

| Tuesday |
|---|
|  |

| Wednesday |
|---|
|  |

| Thursday |
|---|
|  |

| Friday |
|---|
|  |

| Saturday |
|---|
|  |

Week of: _____

## Goals

1. _____
2. _____
3. _____
4. _____

## To-Do

○ _____
○ _____
○ _____
○ _____
○ _____
○ _____
○ _____
○ _____

## Notes

_____
_____
_____
_____

# Weekly Plan

| | |
|---|---|
| Sunday | |
| Monday | |
| Tuesday | |
| Wednesday | |
| Thursday | |
| Friday | |
| Saturday | |

Week of: _____

## Goals

1. _____
2. _____
3. _____
4. _____

## To-Do

○ _____
○ _____
○ _____
○ _____
○ _____
○ _____
○ _____
○ _____

## Notes

_____
_____
_____
_____

# Weekly Plan

| | |
|---|---|
| **Sunday** | |
| **Monday** | |
| **Tuesday** | |
| **Wednesday** | |
| **Thursday** | |
| **Friday** | |
| **Saturday** | |

Week of: _____

## Goals

1. _____
2. _____
3. _____
4. _____

## To-Do

- ○ _____
- ○ _____
- ○ _____
- ○ _____
- ○ _____
- ○ _____
- ○ _____
- ○ _____

## Notes

_____
_____
_____
_____

Date:

How was visit with your love one?

_____

_____

_____

_____

_____

_____

_____

_____

_____

_____

_____

_____

_____

_____

_____

_____

Date:

How was visit with your love one?

_____

_____

_____

_____

_____

_____

_____

_____

_____

_____

_____

_____

_____

_____

_____

_____

# my prayer
## LIST

*family*

_____
_____
_____
_____

*friends*

_____
_____
_____
_____

*neighbors*

_____
_____
_____
_____

*self*

_____
_____
_____
_____

# Birthdays
# &
# Anniversaries

# JANUARY.

- [ ] _____
- [ ] _____
- [ ] _____
- [ ] _____
- [ ] _____
- [ ] _____
- [ ] _____
- [ ] _____

# February

- [ ] _____
- [ ] _____
- [ ] _____
- [ ] _____
- [ ] _____
- [ ] _____
- [ ] _____
- [ ] _____

# March

- [ ] _____
- [ ] _____
- [ ] _____
- [ ] _____
- [ ] _____
- [ ] _____
- [ ] _____
- [ ] _____

# april.

- [ ] _____
- [ ] _____
- [ ] _____
- [ ] _____
- [ ] _____
- [ ] _____
- [ ] _____
- [ ] _____

# may

- [ ] _____
- [ ] _____
- [ ] _____
- [ ] _____
- [ ] _____
- [ ] _____
- [ ] _____
- [ ] _____

# june

- [ ] _____
- [ ] _____
- [ ] _____
- [ ] _____
- [ ] _____
- [ ] _____
- [ ] _____
- [ ] _____

# JULY.

- [ ] _____
- [ ] _____
- [ ] _____
- [ ] _____
- [ ] _____
- [ ] _____
- [ ] _____
- [ ] _____

# August

- [ ] _____
- [ ] _____
- [ ] _____
- [ ] _____
- [ ] _____
- [ ] _____
- [ ] _____
- [ ] _____

# September

- [ ] _____
- [ ] _____
- [ ] _____
- [ ] _____
- [ ] _____
- [ ] _____
- [ ] _____
- [ ] _____

# October

- [ ] _____
- [ ] _____
- [ ] _____
- [ ] _____
- [ ] _____
- [ ] _____
- [ ] _____
- [ ] _____

# November

- [ ] _____
- [ ] _____
- [ ] _____
- [ ] _____
- [ ] _____
- [ ] _____
- [ ] _____
- [ ] _____

# December

- [ ] _____
- [ ] _____
- [ ] _____
- [ ] _____
- [ ] _____
- [ ] _____
- [ ] _____
- [ ] _____

# extras

- [ ] _____
- [ ] _____
- [ ] _____
- [ ] _____
- [ ] _____
- [ ] _____
- [ ] _____
- [ ] _____

- [ ] _____
- [ ] _____
- [ ] _____
- [ ] _____
- [ ] _____
- [ ] _____
- [ ] _____
- [ ] _____

- [ ] _____
- [ ] _____
- [ ] _____
- [ ] _____
- [ ] _____
- [ ] _____
- [ ] _____
- [ ] _____

- [ ] _____
- [ ] _____
- [ ] _____
- [ ] _____
- [ ] _____
- [ ] _____
- [ ] _____
- [ ] _____

# friends & family

## CONTACTS

Name_____

Street Address_____

City: _____State: _____Zip Code: _____

Home Phone: _____ Cell Phone: _____

Work Phone: _____ Email: _____

====================================================

Name_____

Street Address_____

City: _____State: _____Zip Code: _____

Home Phone: _____ Cell Phone: _____

Work Phone: _____ Email: _____

====================================================

Name_____

Street Address_____

City: _____State: _____Zip Code: _____

Home Phone: _____ Cell Phone: _____

Work Phone: _____ Email: _____

Name_____

Street Address_____

City: _____State: _____Zip Code: _____

Home Phone: _____ Cell Phone: _____

Work Phone: _____ Email: _____

========================================================

Name_____

Street Address_____

City: _____State: _____Zip Code: _____

Home Phone: _____ Cell Phone: _____

Work Phone: _____ Email: _____

========================================================

Name_____

Street Address_____

City: _____State: _____Zip Code: _____

Home Phone: _____ Cell Phone: _____

Work Phone: _____ Email: _____

Name_____

Street Address_____

City: _____State: _____Zip Code: _____

Home Phone: _____ Cell Phone: _____

Work Phone: _____ Email: _____

Name_____

Street Address_____

City: _____State: _____Zip Code: _____

Home Phone: _____ Cell Phone: _____

Work Phone: _____ Email: _____

Name_____

Street Address_____

City: _____State: _____Zip Code: _____

Home Phone: _____ Cell Phone: _____

Work Phone: _____ Email: _____

Name_____

Street Address_____

City: _____State: _____Zip Code: _____

Home Phone: _____ Cell Phone: _____

Work Phone: _____ Email: _____

Name_____

Street Address_____

City: _____State: _____Zip Code: _____

Home Phone: _____ Cell Phone: _____

Work Phone: _____ Email: _____

Name_____

Street Address_____

City: _____State: _____Zip Code: _____

Home Phone: _____ Cell Phone: _____

Work Phone: _____ Email: _____

Name_____

Street Address_____

City: _____State: _____Zip Code: _____

Home Phone: _____ Cell Phone: _____

Work Phone: _____ Email: _____

═══════════════════════════════════════════════════

Name_____

Street Address_____

City: _____State: _____Zip Code: _____

Home Phone: _____ Cell Phone: _____

Work Phone: _____ Email: _____

═══════════════════════════════════════════════════

Name_____

Street Address_____

City: _____State: _____Zip Code: _____

Home Phone: _____ Cell Phone: _____

Work Phone: _____ Email: _____

Name_____

Street Address_____

City: _____State: _____Zip Code: _____

Home Phone: _____ Cell Phone: _____

Work Phone: _____ Email: _____

═══════════════════════════════════════════════

Name_____

Street Address_____

City: _____State: _____Zip Code: _____

Home Phone: _____ Cell Phone: _____

Work Phone: _____ Email: _____

═══════════════════════════════════════════════

Name_____

Street Address_____

City: _____State: _____Zip Code: _____

Home Phone: _____ Cell Phone: _____

Work Phone: _____ Email: _____

We are Mr. and Mrs. Shervon "Goldie" Johnson.  Currently he is incarcerated at Northeast Correctional Complex in Tennessee and he has been incarcerated since 1995. He is currently serving a 70 year sentence for attempted 1st degree murder, aggravated robbery and attempted aggravated robbery. He was also indicted in the US District Court for the same incidents under the Hobbs Act Robbery. He has been serving excessive time since the age of 22 in the state of Tennessee. Since Shervon, I have grown to love this man beyond measure, through the highs and lows.

Shervon is a man that the Creator of the heavens and earth has set apart to be and do good deeds. What I have learned from my husband is the true meaning of friendship, faith, patience, loyalty and unconditional shameless love.

Colossians 3:10 and you have become a new person. This new person is continually renewed in knowledge to be like its Creator.

Ephesians 2:10 for we are The Creator of heavens and earth masterpiece. He has created us anew in His Son name, so we can do the good things he planned for us long ago.

# ALL BECAUSE TWO PEOPLE

## FELL IN *Love*

And finally stay in the WORD *together* the more intimate you are with THE CREATOR OF THE HEAVENS AND EARTH, the more intimate and closer your relationship becomes. I know this from experience. This journey that we're on takes unconditional love. We have good days and bad days, but we understand we can only work if we are dedicated to one another despite any worldly distractions. Care enough for each other to eliminate all doubt and insecurities and everything will be alright. I've been by his side now going on 3 years, my husband values me, understands me and appreciates me. I pray to all that received this journal that your life be filled with miracles, breakthroughs, good news, abundance and love. More importantly, I pray THE CREATOR OF THE HEAVENS AND EARTH will make all things beautiful for you and yours.

INCARCERATED

Made in the USA
Las Vegas, NV
20 October 2024

10091411R00098